TSK'S TOEFL VOCABULARY BUILDER

Colette Smith and Nicola Porter

Taraska Press

LEARNING
TOOLS
TARASKA PRESS

CONTENTS

PREFACE

This book is purely to support students undertaking the TOEFL test.

WELCOME TO TSK'S TOEFL VOCABULARY BUILDER

T his comprehensive vocabulary book provided here offers an excellent resource for TOEFL preparation, enabling students to enhance their vocabulary skills and improve their performance on the exam. Here's a guide on how to effectively utilize this book:

1. Familiarize yourself with the book: Begin by familiarizing yourself with the structure and organization of the book. Take note of the different groups or sections, as well as the accompanying word lists and example sentences.

2. Assess your current vocabulary level: Before diving into the book, assess your current vocabulary level. This will help you identify areas of strength and areas that require more focus. It will also allow you to gauge your progress as you work through the book.

3. Set study goals: Establish study goals that align with your target TOEFL score and timeframe. Break down your goals into manageable chunks, such as completing a certain number of groups or sections each week. This

will help you stay organized and motivated throughout your study journey. Study one group at a time.

4. Approach the book one group at a time. Start with Group 1 and work your way through systematically. Within each group, focus on the word meanings, example sentences, and the provided options for each word.

5. Practice with revision tests: As you study each group, engage in the revision tests provided earlier. These tests will reinforce your understanding of the words, challenge your recall, and improve your ability to select the correct word in context. Remember to review the explanations for the correct answers to solidify your knowledge.

6. Create flashcards or word lists: As you encounter new words, consider creating flashcards or word lists for further review. Include the word, its meanings, example sentences, and any additional notes you find helpful. Regularly review these flashcards or word lists to reinforce your learning.

7. Apply the words in context: Practice using the words in context by incorporating them into your daily activities. Read English literature, news articles, or academic texts to see how the words are used naturally. Try to incorporate them into your writing and speaking practice as well.

8. Monitor progress and review: Regularly assess your progress by revisiting previously studied groups. Use the revision tests or re-read the example sentences to ensure you retain the knowledge. Identify any areas that need further reinforcement and dedicate additional time to reviewing those words.

9. Supplement with other study materials: While this vocabulary book is a valuable resource, remember to supplement your study with other TOEFL materials. Engage in reading comprehension exercises, listening practice, and essay writing to develop a well-rounded

skill set for the exam.

10. Stay consistent and motivated: Consistency is key in vocabulary learning. Set aside dedicated study time each day or week and stick to your schedule. Keep yourself motivated by tracking your progress, celebrating milestones, and visualizing your success on the TOEFL.

By following this approach, using the book as a comprehensive resource, and incorporating regular practice, you can effectively enhance your vocabulary skills and boost your performance on the TOEFL exam. Remember, building a strong vocabulary takes time and persistence!

THE 500 WORDS YOU MUST KNOW!

Studying vocabulary is an essential part of preparing for the TOEFL exam, as it helps you understand and communicate effectively in English. The lists of words provided here can be valuable resources for expanding your vocabulary and improving your chances of achieving a good TOEFL score. Here are some tips on how to make the most of these word lists:

1. Familiarize yourself with the words: Take the time to go through each group of words and read the definitions carefully. Pay attention to the correct meanings of the words and their usage in example sentences.

2. Test your understanding: After going through a group of words, cover up the definitions and try to recall the correct meaning for each word. Use the multiple-choice options provided to test your knowledge. This will help reinforce your understanding and improve your ability to recognize the words in different contexts.

3. Use the words in context: Understanding the meaning of a word is important, but being able to use it correctly in a sentence is equally crucial. Practice using the words in your own sentences to ensure you can apply them

appropriately.

4. Create flashcards or word lists: Write down the words and their correct meanings on flashcards or create a separate word list. Review them regularly and test yourself to reinforce your memory and understanding. You can also group the words based on their themes or similarities to aid in memorization.

5. Expand your knowledge: While these word lists provide a solid foundation, don't limit your vocabulary study to just these words. Explore additional resources such as textbooks, online vocabulary exercises, and English language websites to broaden your knowledge and exposure to different word contexts.

6. Practice with TOEFL-style questions: As you progress in your vocabulary study, it's essential to practice using the words in the context of TOEFL-style questions. Solve practice exercises and sample questions that require you to comprehend and apply the vocabulary in reading, listening, speaking, and writing tasks.

Remember, building vocabulary is a gradual process, so make a study plan and allocate dedicated time each day to review and practice. Aim for consistency and actively incorporate these words into your daily English usage. With regular practice and exposure, you will become more confident and proficient in using the words effectively, which will significantly benefit your TOEFL performance. Good luck with your studies!

Group 1:

Abate:

    a) To intensify

    b) To reduce

    c) To emphasize

Example sentence: The storm began to abate, and the wind slowly died down.

Benevolent:

    a) Friendly

    b) Hostile

    c) Indifferent

Example sentence: The benevolent old woman donated her entire savings to the orphanage.

Coalesce:

    a) To combine

    b) To separate

    c) To demolish

Example sentence: The two political parties decided to coalesce and form a coalition government.

Deft:

    a) Clumsy

    b) Skillful

    c) Careless

Example sentence: The pianist's deft fingers moved gracefully across the keys.

Egregious:

    a) Outstanding

    b) Shocking

    c) Mediocre

Example sentence: The politician's behavior was so egregious that it led to public outrage.

Fallacious:

a) Accurate

b) Misleading

c) Sincere

Example sentence: The argument put forward by the speaker was fallacious and lacked evidence.

Gregarious:

a) Sociable

b) Introverted

c) Aggressive

Example sentence: John is a gregarious person who enjoys being around large groups of friends.

Hierarchy:

a) Equality

b) Power structure

c) Anarchy

Example sentence: The CEO is at the top of the corporate hierarchy.

Impartial:

a) Biased

b) Neutral

c) Judgmental

Example sentence: The judge remained impartial throughout the trial, considering all the evidence.

Jeopardize:

a) To protect

b) To endanger

c) To enhance

Example sentence: His reckless behavior could jeopardize

the success of the entire project.

Group 2:

Kindle:

    a) To extinguish

    b) To ignite

    c) To conceal

Example sentence: She used a match to kindle the fire in the fireplace.

Lethargic:

    a) Energetic

    b) Active

    c) Sluggish

Example sentence: After a heavy meal, he felt lethargic and didn't want to move.

Mitigate:

    a) To intensify

    b) To worsen

    c) To alleviate

Example sentence: The government implemented measures to mitigate the effects of the economic crisis.

Nostalgia:

    a) Longing for the past

    b) Anticipation of the future

    c) Indifference to time

Example sentence: As she flipped through her old photo album, a wave of nostalgia washed over her.

Ominous:

    a) Promising

    b) Threatening

    c) Fortunate

Example sentence: The dark clouds and rumbling thunder were ominous signs of an approaching storm.

Prolific:

a) Productive

b) Lazy

c) Ineffective

Example sentence: The renowned author was known for her prolific output of novels.

Quell:

a) To provoke

b) To calm

c) To intensify

Example sentence: The police tried to quell the riot by using tear gas.

Reciprocate:

a) To reject

b) To repay

c) To ignore

Example sentence: If someone does you a favor, it's polite to reciprocate the kindness.

Salient:

a) Prominent

b) Hidden

c) Insignificant

Example sentence: The speaker highlighted the most salient points of his argument.

Trepidation:

a) Fear

b) Confidence

c) Indifference

Example sentence: She approached the haunted house with

trepidation, unsure of what awaited her inside.

Group 3:

Alleviate:

    a) To worsen

    b) To mitigate

    c) To complicate

Example sentence: The medication helped to alleviate her pain and discomfort.

Belligerent:

    a) Peaceful

    b) Aggressive

    c) Cooperative

Example sentence: The belligerent man started a fight with anyone who disagreed with him.

Concise:

    a) Lengthy

    b) Brief

    c) Elaborate

Example sentence: The professor gave a concise explanation of the complex theory.

Derive:

    a) To invent

    b) To originate

    c) To destroy

Example sentence: The word "alphabet" derives from the Greek letters "alpha" and "beta."

Enigma:

    a) Mystery

    b) Clarity

    c) Obviousness

Example sentence: The disappearance of the famous artist remains an enigma to this day.

Fickle:

a) Reliable

b) Inconsistent

c) Steadfast

Example sentence: Mary is known for her fickle nature; her preferences change frequently.

Gratify:

a) To disappoint

b) To satisfy

c) To disregard

Example sentence: Winning the championship gratified the team and their dedicated fans.

Hypothetical:

a) Imaginary

b) Concrete

c) Actual

Example sentence: Let's consider a hypothetical situation to explore different possibilities.

Impede:

a) To accelerate

b) To obstruct

c) To facilitate

Example sentence: The heavy traffic impeded their progress towards the airport.

Juxtapose:

a) To separate

b) To compare

c) To ignore

Example sentence: The artist juxtaposed vibrant colors

with dark shadows in her painting.

Group 4:

Acumen:

    a) Ignorance

    b) Insight

    c) Indifference

Example sentence: The successful entrepreneur had a keen business acumen.

Bolster:

    a) To weaken

    b) To support

    c) To abandon

Example sentence: The evidence presented in court bolstered the prosecutor's case.

Concur:

    a) To disagree

    b) To approve

    c) To doubt

Example sentence: The committee members concurred on the need for stricter regulations.

Delineate:

    a) To erase

    b) To outline

    c) To confuse

Example sentence: The teacher used a whiteboard to delineate the steps of the scientific process.

Eloquent:

    a) Articulate

    b) Incoherent

    c) Mute

Example sentence: The politician delivered an eloquent speech that moved the audience.

Frivolous:

a) Serious

b) Trivial

c) Essential

Example sentence: The judge dismissed the frivolous lawsuit, deeming it without merit.

Hackneyed:

a) Fresh

b) Original

c) Clichéd

Example sentence: The writer avoided using hackneyed phrases and sought innovative expressions.

Incessant:

a) Continuous

b) Sporadic

c) Intermittent

Example sentence: The incessant rain made it difficult to go outside.

Jeopardy:

a) Safety

b) Risk

c) Security

Example sentence: The hiker put himself in jeopardy by venturing into the dangerous terrain alone.

Lament:

a) To celebrate

b) To mourn

c) To applaud

Example sentence: The poet wrote a heartfelt poem to

lament the loss of a loved one.

Group 5:

Acquiesce:

  a) To resist

  b) To comply

  c) To challenge

Example sentence: Despite her disagreement, she eventually acquiesced to her friend's request.

Brevity:

  a) Lengthiness

  b) Conciseness

  c) Elaboration

Example sentence: The speaker delivered his message with brevity, keeping the presentation short and concise.

Conscientious:

  a) Careless

  b) Diligent

  c) Negligent

Example sentence: The conscientious student always completed her assignments on time.

Discern:

  a) To confuse

  b) To perceive

  c) To ignore

Example sentence: It can be difficult to discern the true intentions behind someone's words.

Eminent:

  a) Unknown

  b) Prominent

  c) Insignificant

Example sentence: The renowned scientist was considered an eminent figure in his field.

Frugal:

a) Extravagant

b) Economical

c) Wasteful

Example sentence: She lived a frugal lifestyle, carefully managing her expenses.

Harbinger:

a) Messenger

b) Omen

c) Disregard

Example sentence: The first robin of spring is often seen as a harbinger of warmer weather.

Incite:

a) To provoke

b) To pacify

c) To soothe

Example sentence: The speaker's passionate words incited the crowd to take action.

Jovial:

a) Gloomy

b) Merry

c) Solemn

Example sentence: The party was filled with jovial laughter and cheerful conversations.

Laudable:

a) Blameworthy

b) Praiseworthy

c) Disgraceful

Example sentence: Her efforts to raise funds for charity

were laudable and admirable.

Group 6:

Adversary:

   a) Ally

   b) Foe

   c) Colleague

Example sentence: In the courtroom, the defense attorney challenged the arguments presented by the adversary.

Capricious:

   a) Predictable

   b) Impulsive

   c) Rational

Example sentence: Her capricious nature made it difficult to anticipate her actions.

Deficit:

   a) Surplus

   b) Shortfall

   c) Excess

Example sentence: The company's financial report showed a significant deficit for the past fiscal year.

Elucidate:

   a) To confuse

   b) To clarify

   c) To distort

Example sentence: The professor used diagrams to elucidate the complex scientific concept.

Enthrall:

   a) To bore

   b) To captivate

   c) To ignore

Example sentence: The magician's performance enthralled the audience, leaving them amazed.

Futile:

a) Successful

b) Pointless

c) Effective

Example sentence: Despite his efforts, his attempts to fix the broken vase were futile.

Haughty:

a) Humble

b) Arrogant

c) Modest

Example sentence: The haughty millionaire looked down upon those who were less wealthy.

Incognito:

a) Visible

b) Disguised

c) Exposed

Example sentence: The celebrity tried to go incognito by wearing a hat and sunglasses.

Lethargy:

a) Energy

b) Laziness

c) Enthusiasm

Example sentence: After a long day at work, he felt a sense of lethargy and lacked motivation.

Meticulous:

a) Careful

b) Careless

c) Hasty

Example sentence: The painter was meticulous in her

attention to detail, ensuring every brushstroke was precise.

Group 7:

Advocate:

    a) Oppose

    b) Support

    c) Ignore

Example sentence: The activist passionately advocated for equal rights.

Catalyst:

    a) Hindrance

    b) Stimulus

    c) Barrier

Example sentence: The new technology acted as a catalyst for economic growth.

Diverse:

    a) Homogeneous

    b) Varied

    c) Identical

Example sentence: The school prides itself on its diverse student population.

Emulate:

    a) Imitate

    b) Disregard

    c) Deviate

Example sentence: Aspiring artists often try to emulate the techniques of their favorite painters.

Exacerbate:

    a) Alleviate

    b) Aggravate

    c) Diminish

Example sentence: His harsh words only served to exacerbate the situation.

Gracious:

    a) Rude

    b) Polite

    c) Impolite

Example sentence: The host welcomed the guests with a gracious smile and warm hospitality.

Hypocrite:

    a) Sincere person

    b) Fraud

    c) Honest individual

Example sentence: The politician's actions were seen as hypocritical, contradicting his public statements.

Indifferent:

    a) Caring

    b) Apathetic

    c) Concerned

Example sentence: She remained indifferent to the outcome of the game, as she wasn't a fan of either team.

Labyrinth:

    a) Straightforward path

    b) Maze

    c) Simple route

Example sentence: Navigating through the old castle's labyrinth was a challenging task.

Mitigate:

    a) Intensify

    b) Alleviate

    c) Exacerbate

Example sentence: Planting trees can help mitigate the

effects of air pollution.

Group 8:

Aesthetic:

    a) Beautiful

    b) Ugly

    c) Dull

Example sentence: The artwork was praised for its aesthetic appeal and artistic expression.

Coherent:

    a) Incoherent

    b) Logical

    c) Confusing

Example sentence: The professor delivered a coherent lecture, presenting ideas in a clear and organized manner.

Depict:

    a) Conceal

    b) Portray

    c) Suppress

Example sentence: The artist used vibrant colors to depict the beauty of the sunset.

Erratic:

    a) Consistent

    b) Unpredictable

    c) Stable

Example sentence: His erratic behavior raised concerns among his friends and family.

Exemplify:

    a) Deviate

    b) Illustrate

    c) Obstruct

Example sentence: The student's exceptional grades exemplify her dedication to her studies.

Guile:

a) Honesty

b) Deception

c) Sincerity

Example sentence: The con artist used his guile to trick unsuspecting victims.

Incumbent:

a) Former

b) Current

c) Outgoing

Example sentence: The incumbent president is seeking re-election for another term.

Induce:

a) Discourage

b) Persuade

c) Dissuade

Example sentence: The doctor prescribed medication to induce sleep.

Lampoon:

a) Praise

b) Ridicule

c) Compliment

Example sentence: The satirical cartoonist enjoyed lampooning politicians in his drawings.

Morose:

a) Cheerful

b) Gloomy

c) Happy

Example sentence: He appeared morose after receiving the

disappointing news.

Group 9:

Affable:

    a) Unfriendly

    b) Friendly

    c) Hostile

Example sentence: The host was known for his affable personality, making guests feel welcome.

Cogent:

    a) Convincing

    b) Incoherent

    c) Confusing

Example sentence: The lawyer presented a cogent argument that swayed the jury.

Deprive:

    a) Provide

    b) Deny

    c) Fulfill

Example sentence: The storm deprived the town of electricity for several days.

Evoke:

    a) Suppress

    b) Provoke

    c) Quell

Example sentence: The song lyrics evoked feelings of nostalgia and longing.

Exorbitant:

    a) Reasonable

    b) Excessive

    c) Moderate

Example sentence: The price of the luxury car was exorbitant, far beyond most people's budgets.

Hinder:

a) Assist

b) Obstruct

c) Facilitate

Example sentence: The heavy rain hindered their progress during the hike.

Indulge:

a) Deny

b) Gratify

c) Abstain

Example sentence: She decided to indulge in a decadent piece of chocolate cake.

Infallible:

a) Perfect

b) Flawless

c) Fallible

Example sentence: Despite his confidence, no one is infallible and immune to making mistakes.

Lucid:

a) Confusing

b) Clear

c) Ambiguous

Example sentence: The author's lucid writing style made the complex topic easy to understand.

Nostalgia:

a) Remorse

b) Longing

c) Apathy

Example sentence: Looking at old photographs filled her

with nostalgia for her childhood.

Group 10:

Altruistic:

 a) Selfish

 b) Selfless

 c) Greedy

Example sentence: The philanthropist's altruistic acts helped improve the lives of many.

Collateral:

 a) Direct

 b) Indirect

 c) Parallel

Example sentence: The car loan required the borrower to provide collateral in the form of a property.

Derogatory:

 a) Respectful

 b) Insulting

 c) Complimentary

Example sentence: The comedian's derogatory jokes offended some members of the audience.

Erroneous:

 a) Accurate

 b) Incorrect

 c) Precise

Example sentence: The article contained several erroneous statements that needed correction.

Exquisite:

 a) Common

 b) Beautiful

 c) Mediocre

Example sentence: The restaurant served exquisite dishes

prepared by a renowned chef.

Hone:

    a) Dull

    b) Sharpen

    c) Polish

Example sentence: The musician practiced for hours to hone her piano-playing skills.

Indignant:

    a) Pleased

    b) Angry

    c) Content

Example sentence: She became indignant when she discovered her work had been plagiarized.

Infamous:

    a) Unknown

    b) Notorious

    c) Respectable

Example sentence: The town's abandoned building was infamous for its ghostly sightings.

Luminous:

    a) Bright

    b) Dim

    c) Dull

Example sentence: The full moon cast a luminous glow over the tranquil lake.

Novice:

    a) Expert

    b) Beginner

    c) Veteran

Example sentence: As a novice climber, she sought guidance from experienced mountaineers.

Group 11:

Ambiguous:

    a) Clear

    b) Uncertain

    c) Explicit

Example sentence: The ambiguous statement left room for interpretation.

Complacent:

    a) Satisfied

    b) Content

    c) Dissatisfied

Example sentence: The team's complacent attitude led to their downfall.

Desolate:

    a) Populated

    b) Empty

    c) Crowded

Example sentence: The abandoned house stood in the desolate neighborhood.

Esoteric:

    a) Common

    b) Obscure

    c) Familiar

Example sentence: The professor shared esoteric knowledge with his advanced students.

Expedite:

    a) Delay

    b) Accelerate

    c) Hinder

Example sentence: The manager hired additional staff to

expedite the completion of the project.

Impeccable:

    a) Flawless

    b) Imperfect

    c) Faulty

Example sentence: The pianist's performance was impeccable, impressing the entire audience.

Indispensable:

    a) Replaceable

    b) Essential

    c) Optional

Example sentence: The computer has become an indispensable tool in modern society.

Intrepid:

    a) Fearful

    b) Brave

    c) Timid

Example sentence: The intrepid explorer ventured into the uncharted jungle.

Lethal:

    a) Harmless

    b) Deadly

    c) Safe

Example sentence: The venom of the snake is lethal to its prey.

Obscure:

    a) Clear

    b) Unknown

    c) Evident

Example sentence: The writer's early works remained obscure until after his death.

Group 12:

Ambivalent:

  a) Indifferent

  b) Undecided

  c) Determined

  Example sentence: She felt ambivalent about accepting the job offer.

Concise:

  a) Lengthy

  b) Succinct

  c) Wordy

  Example sentence: The professor requested concise answers on the exam.

Destitute:

  a) Wealthy

  b) Impoverished

  c) Affluent

  Example sentence: The homeless man was destitute and had nowhere to go.

Exquisite:

  a) Ordinary

  b) Beautiful

  c) Average

  Example sentence: The jewelry shop showcased exquisite diamond necklaces.

Extol:

  a) Criticize

  b) Praise

  c) Disparage

  Example sentence: The coach extolled the team's effort and

dedication.

Inevitable:

    a) Avoidable

    b) Unavoidable

    c) Optional

    Example sentence: Change is inevitable and part of life's natural process.

Infallible:

    a) Perfect

    b) Flawless

    c) Fallible

    Example sentence: Despite his confidence, no one is infallible and immune to making mistakes.

Intricate:

    a) Simple

    b) Complex

    c) Basic

    Example sentence: The artist's painting showcased intricate details and patterns.

Levity:

    a) Seriousness

    b) Humor

    c) Solemnity

    Example sentence: The comedian's jokes brought levity to the tense atmosphere.

Ominous:

    a) Promising

    b) Threatening

    c) Encouraging

    Example sentence: The dark clouds were an ominous sign of an approaching storm.

Group 13:

Analogous:

    a) Similar

    b) Different

    c) Contrasting

Example sentence: The relationship between the two concepts is analogous to that of siblings.

Condone:

    a) Forgive

    b) Approve

    c) Condemn

Example sentence: The principal cannot condone such behavior in the school.

Deter:

    a) Encourage

    b) Discourage

    c) Motivate

Example sentence: The security measures are meant to deter potential thieves.

Fabricate:

    a) Invent

    b) Destroy

    c) Reveal

Example sentence: The witness admitted to fabricating the story to protect his friend.

Exuberant:

    a) Energetic

    b) Lively

    c) Dull

Example sentence: The children were exuberant and filled

the room with laughter.

Inherent:

a) Acquired

b) Innate

c) Learned

Example sentence: The artist's talent seemed inherent from a young age.

Innocuous:

a) Harmful

b) Safe

c) Dangerous

Example sentence: The spider appeared innocuous, but it was actually venomous.

Intrigue:

a) Bore

b) Fascinate

c) Repel

Example sentence: The mystery novel intrigued readers with its unpredictable plot.

Meager:

a) Abundant

b) Scarce

c) Plentiful

Example sentence: The salary was meager, barely enough to cover the basic expenses.

Ornate:

a) Plain

b) Elaborate

c) Simple

Example sentence: The cathedral's interior featured ornate stained glass windows.

Group 14:

Anecdote:

a) Joke

b) Story

c) Fact

Example sentence: The professor shared an interesting anecdote from his travels.

Conform:

a) Comply

b) Rebel

c) Differ

Example sentence: The students were expected to conform to the school's dress code.

Detrimental:

a) Beneficial

b) Harmful

c) Advantageous

Example sentence: Smoking is detrimental to one's health.

Facilitate:

a) Hinder

b) Assist

c) Complicate

Example sentence: The new software will facilitate the process of data analysis.

Exacerbate:

a) Alleviate

b) Aggravate

c) Diminish

Example sentence: His harsh words only served to exacerbate the situation.

Inquisitive:

    a) Curious

    b) Indifferent

    c) Apathetic

Example sentence: The young child had an inquisitive nature, always asking questions.

Insightful:

    a) Perceptive

    b) Ignorant

    c) Naive

Example sentence: The professor provided insightful analysis of the novel's themes.

Intrude:

    a) Enter

    b) Trespass

    c) Exit

Example sentence: The neighbor apologized for intruding on their private conversation.

Mediocre:

    a) Excellent

    b) Average

    c) Outstanding

Example sentence: The restaurant received mediocre reviews for its food quality.

Ostentatious:

    a) Modest

    b) Showy

    c) Simple

Example sentence: The wealthy businessman displayed his wealth through ostentatious displays of luxury.

Group 15:

Animosity:

    a) Friendliness

    b) Hostility

    c) Harmony

Example sentence: The long-standing animosity between the two rival teams was evident.

Congenial:

    a) Pleasant

    b) Unpleasant

    c) Disagreeable

Example sentence: The hostess greeted her guests with a congenial smile.

Deviate:

    a) Conform

    b) Stray

    c) Comply

Example sentence: He chose to deviate from the traditional approach and took a different path.

Fallacy:

    a) Truth

    b) Error

    c) Accuracy

Example sentence: The argument was based on a logical fallacy and lacked evidence.

Exhilarating:

    a) Boring

    b) Thrilling

    c) Monotonous

Example sentence: The roller coaster ride was exhilarating,

with its twists and turns.

Insight:

    a) Understanding

    b) Ignorance

    c) Stupidity

Example sentence: The therapist provided valuable insights into the patient's behavior.

Intuition:

    a) Reasoning

    b) Instinct

    c) Logic

Example sentence: Her intuition told her that something was not right.

Melancholy:

    a) Joyful

    b) Sad

    c) Happy

Example sentence: The old photograph filled her with a sense of melancholy.

Ostracize:

    a) Include

    b) Exclude

    c) Embrace

Example sentence: The group decided to ostracize the member who broke the rules.

Pensive:

    a) Thoughtful

    b) Carefree

    c) Distracted

Example sentence: She sat by the window, lost in pensive reflection.

Group 16:

Annex:

    a) Detach

    b) Add

    c) Remove

Example sentence: The country annexed the neighboring territory.

Connotation:

    a) Denotation

    b) Implication

    c) Definition

Example sentence: The word "home" has a positive connotation for most people.

Devoid:

    a) Empty

    b) Full

    c) Abundant

Example sentence: The room was devoid of furniture and decorations.

Fanatic:

    a) Enthusiast

    b) Extremist

    c) Moderate

Example sentence: The soccer fanatic never missed a game and collected memorabilia.

Exonerate:

    a) Clear

    b) Convict

    c) Incriminate

Example sentence: The new evidence exonerated the

defendant, proving his innocence.

Instigate:

    a) Initiate

    b) Prevent

    c) Discourage

Example sentence: The article instigated a lively debate among the readers.

Intervene:

    a) Meddle

    b) Interfere

    c) Ignore

Example sentence: The teacher had to intervene and separate the fighting students.

Mercenary:

    a) Greedy

    b) Selfless

    c) Altruistic

Example sentence: The mercenary soldier fought for money rather than a cause.

Oust:

    a) Remove

    b) Retain

    c) Retire

Example sentence: The shareholders voted to oust the CEO due to financial misconduct.

Perceptive:

    a) Observant

    b) Oblivious

    c) Unaware

Example sentence: She had a perceptive eye for detail and noticed things others overlooked.

Group 17:

Antagonize:

    a) Provoke

    b) Please

    c) Pacify

Example sentence: The teenager's sarcastic remarks only served to antagonize his parents.

Consensus:

    a) Agreement

    b) Disagreement

    c) Conflict

Example sentence: After much discussion, the committee reached a consensus on the decision.

Devout:

    a) Religious

    b) Impious

    c) Atheistic

Example sentence: The devout followers gathered at the temple for their daily prayers.

Fanfare:

    a) Celebration

    b) Attention

    c) Silence

Example sentence: The grand opening of the store was accompanied by fanfare and excitement.

Expanse:

    a) Stretch

    b) Limitation

    c) Boundary

Example sentence: The vast expanse of the desert extended

as far as the eye could see.

Insurmountable:

    a) Unbeatable

    b) Overcome

    c) Surmountable

Example sentence: The challenges seemed insurmountable, but they persevered.

Intimidate:

    a) Frighten

    b) Encourage

    c) Reassure

Example sentence: The bully used threats to intimidate his classmates.

Meticulous:

    a) Careful

    b) Sloppy

    c) Careless

Example sentence: The artist was meticulous in every brushstroke, ensuring perfection.

Outlandish:

    a) Strange

    b) Normal

    c) Conventional

Example sentence: The actress wore an outlandish outfit to the award ceremony.

Pessimistic:

    a) Negative

    b) Optimistic

    c) Hopeful

Example sentence: Despite the setbacks, she remained pessimistic about the project's success.

Group 18:

Anticipate:

    a) Expect

    b) Surpass

    c) Disregard

Example sentence: The students eagerly anticipated the announcement of their grades.

Constraint:

    a) Limitation

    b) Freedom

    c) Flexibility

Example sentence: The team worked under the constraint of a tight deadline.

Discern:

    a) Perceive

    b) Ignore

    c) Overlook

Example sentence: It was difficult to discern the truth from the conflicting reports.

Fastidious:

    a) Meticulous

    b) Careless

    c) Negligent

Example sentence: The chef was known for his fastidious attention to detail.

Exploit:

    a) Utilize

    b) Neglect

    c) Ignore

Example sentence: The company sought to exploit new

markets for its products.

Intrepid:

    a) Fearless

    b) Timid

    c) Anxious

Example sentence: The intrepid hiker climbed the treacherous mountain without hesitation.

Intrinsic:

    a) Essential

    b) Extrinsic

    c) Superfluous

Example sentence: Her love for music was intrinsic to her identity.

Misconception:

    a) Fallacy

    b) Correct understanding

    c) Accurate perception

Example sentence: The teacher clarified the misconception about the scientific theory.

Overwhelm:

    a) Overpower

    b) Underwhelm

    c) Underestimate

Example sentence: The sheer number of tasks overwhelmed her, and she felt stressed.

Plausible:

    a) Believable

    b) Implausible

    c) Unconvincing

Example sentence: The detective considered various plausible explanations for the crime.

Group 19:

Apathetic:

a) Indifferent

b) Enthusiastic

c) Passionate

Example sentence: The apathetic audience showed little interest in the speaker's presentation.

Consummate:

a) Skilled

b) Incomplete

c) Mediocre

Example sentence: The pianist's performance was consummate, showcasing mastery of the instrument.

Dismantle:

a) Take apart

b) Assemble

c) Construct

Example sentence: The mechanic dismantled the engine to identify the problem.

Expunge:

a) Erase

b) Preserve

c) Retain

Example sentence: The court ordered the criminal record to be expunged after the rehabilitation.

Intuition:

a) Gut feeling

b) Logic

c) Rationality

Example sentence: Her intuition guided her to make the

right decision.

Inundate:

    a) Flood

    b) Drought

    c) Drain

Example sentence: The heavy rain inundated the streets, causing widespread flooding.

Mitigate:

    a) Alleviate

    b) Aggravate

    c) Intensify

Example sentence: The organization implemented measures to mitigate the impact of climate change.

Paramount:

    a) Crucial

    b) Insignificant

    c) Irrelevant

Example sentence: The safety of the passengers was of paramount importance.

Overwhelming:

    a) Enormous

    b) Manageable

    c) Moderate

Example sentence: The team faced overwhelming odds but managed to achieve victory.

Ponder:

    a) Contemplate

    b) Disregard

    c) Ignore

Example sentence: She sat by the fireplace, pondering the meaning of life.

Group 20:

Apprehensive:

    a) Anxious

    b) Confident

    c) Reassured

Example sentence: The student felt apprehensive before taking the final exam.

Contend:

    a) Compete

    b) Surrender

    c) Yield

Example sentence: The athletes will contend for the gold medal in the upcoming tournament.

Disparage:

    a) Criticize

    b) Praise

    c) Applaud

Example sentence: She constantly disparaged her colleagues, undermining their confidence.

Extensive:

    a) Vast

    b) Limited

    c) Narrow

Example sentence: The research project required extensive data collection and analysis.

Intricate:

    a) Complex

    b) Simple

    c) Straightforward

Example sentence: The intricate design of the lacework

impressed the onlookers.

Plausible:

    a) Credible

    b) Implausible

    c) Unconvincing

Example sentence: The detective found a plausible explanation for the mysterious disappearance.

Pragmatic:

    a) Practical

    b) Idealistic

    c) Impractical

Example sentence: The pragmatic approach focuses on finding effective solutions.

Paramount:

    a) Crucial

    b) Insignificant

    c) Irrelevant

Example sentence: The safety of the passengers was of paramount importance.

Reconcile:

    a) Resolve

    b) Conflict

    c) Aggravate

Example sentence: The couple sought therapy to reconcile their differences.

Ponder:

    a) Contemplate

    b) Disregard

    c) Ignore

Example sentence: She sat by the fireplace, pondering the meaning of life.

Group 21:

Apprehensive:

a) Anxious

b) Confident

c) Reassured

Example sentence: The student felt apprehensive before taking the final exam.

Contend:

a) Compete

b) Surrender

c) Yield

Example sentence: The athletes will contend for the gold medal in the upcoming tournament.

Disparage:

a) Criticize

b) Praise

c) Applaud

Example sentence: She constantly disparaged her colleagues, undermining their confidence.

Extensive:

a) Vast

b) Limited

c) Narrow

Example sentence: The research project required extensive data collection and analysis.

Intricate:

a) Complex

b) Simple

c) Straightforward

Example sentence: The intricate design of the lacework

impressed the onlookers.

Plausible:

a) Credible

b) Implausible

c) Unconvincing

Example sentence: The detective found a plausible explanation for the mysterious disappearance.

Pragmatic:

a) Practical

b) Idealistic

c) Impractical

Example sentence: The pragmatic approach focuses on finding effective solutions.

Paramount:

a) Crucial

b) Insignificant

c) Irrelevant

Example sentence: The safety of the passengers was of paramount importance.

Reconcile:

a) Resolve

b) Conflict

c) Aggravate

Example sentence: The couple sought therapy to reconcile their differences.

Ponder:

a) Contemplate

b) Disregard

c) Ignore

Example sentence: She sat by the fireplace, pondering the meaning of life.

Group 22:

Alleviate:

    a) Relieve

    b) Aggravate

    c) Intensify

    Example sentence: The medication helped alleviate her pain.

Convey:

    a) Communicate

    b) Conceal

    c) Withhold

    Example sentence: He used gestures to convey his message to the audience.

Dissent:

    a) Disagree

    b) Agree

    c) Concur

    Example sentence: The committee members voiced their dissent regarding the proposed policy.

Exuberant:

    a) Energetic

    b) Dull

    c) Lethargic

    Example sentence: The children were exuberant after receiving their presents.

Intrigue:

    a) Fascinate

    b) Bore

    c) Repel

    Example sentence: The mystery novel's plot intrigued the

readers.

Poignant:

    a) Touching

    b) Insignificant

    c) Insensitive

Example sentence: The film's poignant ending left the audience in tears.

Prevalent:

    a) Common

    b) Rare

    c) Unusual

Example sentence: In some cultures, certain superstitions are prevalent.

Relegate:

    a) Demote

    b) Promote

    c) Elevate

Example sentence: The experienced employee was relegated to a lower position due to budget cuts.

Revoke:

    a) Cancel

    b) Grant

    c) Authorize

Example sentence: The government decided to revoke the driver's license due to multiple violations.

Refute:

    a) Disprove

    b) Confirm

    c) Validate

Example sentence: The scientist presented evidence to refute the theory.

Group 23:

Ambiguous:

    a) Unclear

    b) Clear

    c) Distinct

Example sentence: The politician's statement was deliberately ambiguous, leaving room for interpretation.

Condone:

    a) Pardon

    b) Condemn

    c) Criticize

Example sentence: The teacher cannot condone cheating and has a strict policy against it.

Diverse:

    a) Varied

    b) Homogeneous

    c) Uniform

Example sentence: The city is known for its diverse population and multicultural atmosphere.

Feasible:

    a) Possible

    b) Impossible

    c) Impractical

Example sentence: After careful analysis, the project was deemed feasible and worth pursuing.

Invariably:

    a) Always

    b) Occasionally

    c) Rarely

Example sentence: The sunrise at the beach is invariably a

breathtaking sight.

Pristine:

    a) Immaculate

    b) Dirty

    c) Tarnished

Example sentence: The newly renovated house looked pristine and flawless.

Reiterate:

    a) Repeat

    b) Forget

    c) Neglect

Example sentence: The professor reiterated the main points of the lecture for clarification.

Renounce:

    a) Reject

    b) Embrace

    c) Accept

Example sentence: The athlete decided to renounce his title and retire from professional sports.

Resilient:

    a) Strong

    b) Fragile

    c) Weak

Example sentence: Despite facing numerous challenges, she remained resilient and persevered.

Scrutinize:

    a) Examine

    b) Ignore

    c) Neglect

Example sentence: The detective scrutinized the crime scene for any potential evidence.

Group 24:

Ambivalence:

    a) Uncertainty

    b) Certainty

    c) Clarity

Example sentence: She felt ambivalence about accepting the job offer due to conflicting opinions.

Conducive:

    a) Favorable

    b) Detrimental

    c) Harmful

Example sentence: A calm environment is conducive to productive studying.

Divulge:

    a) Disclose

    b) Conceal

    c) Hide

Example sentence: The witness refused to divulge any information about the incident.

Fluctuate:

    a) Vary

    b) Stabilize

    c) Remain constant

Example sentence: The stock prices fluctuated throughout the day.

Inevitable:

    a) Unavoidable

    b) Avoidable

    c) Preventable

Example sentence: Change is inevitable and a part of life.

Prodigy:

    a) Genius

    b) Average

    c) Mediocre

Example sentence: The young pianist was hailed as a prodigy for her exceptional talent.

Reclusive:

    a) Withdrawn

    b) Social

    c) Outgoing

Example sentence: The author lived a reclusive life, rarely interacting with others.

Resolute:

    a) Determined

    b) Indecisive

    c) Vacillating

Example sentence: Despite the obstacles, she remained resolute in achieving her goals.

Skeptical:

    a) Doubtful

    b) Trusting

    c) Credulous

Example sentence: The scientist was skeptical of the new research findings until further evidence was presented.

Scrutiny:

    a) Examination

    b) Neglect

    c) Disregard

Example sentence: The project underwent thorough scrutiny to ensure its accuracy and quality.

Group 25:

Ambivalent:

    a) Indecisive

    b) Decisive

    c) Confident

Example sentence: She felt ambivalent about accepting the job offer due to conflicting opinions.

Conform:

    a) Comply

    b) Rebel

    c) Resist

Example sentence: The students were expected to conform to the school's dress code.

Docile:

    a) Obedient

    b) Rebellious

    c) Defiant

Example sentence: The puppy was docile and easily trained.

Flourish:

    a) Thrive

    b) Wither

    c) Decline

Example sentence: The business began to flourish after implementing a new marketing strategy.

Infer:

    a) Deduce

    b) Misinterpret

    c) Confuse

Example sentence: Based on the evidence, we can infer that he was present at the scene of the crime.

Prolific:

a) Productive

b) Unproductive

c) Lazy

Example sentence: The author has written numerous best-selling books and is known for being prolific.

Reconcile:

a) Resolve

b) Conflict

c) Aggravate

Example sentence: The couple sought therapy to reconcile their differences.

Resolute:

a) Determined

b) Indecisive

c) Vacillating

Example sentence: Despite the obstacles, she remained resolute in achieving her goals.

Skeptical:

a) Doubtful

b) Trusting

c) Credulous

Example sentence: The scientist was skeptical of the new research findings until further evidence was presented.

Scrutiny:

a) Examination

b) Neglect

c) Disregard

Example sentence: The project underwent thorough scrutiny to ensure its accuracy and quality.

Group 26:

Ameliorate:

    a) Improve

    b) Worsen

    c) Deteriorate

Example sentence: The new medication helped ameliorate her symptoms.

Congenial:

    a) Friendly

    b) Unfriendly

    c) Hostile

Example sentence: She found her colleagues to be congenial and easy to work with.

Dogmatic:

    a) Opinionated

    b) Flexible

    c) Open-minded

Example sentence: The professor was known for his dogmatic views on the subject.

Fortuitous:

    a) Lucky

    b) Unfortunate

    c) Unlucky

Example sentence: Winning the lottery was a fortuitous event in his life.

Ingenious:

    a) Clever

    b) Stupid

    c) Dull

Example sentence: The inventor came up with an ingenious

solution to the problem.

Prolong:

a) Extend

b) Shorten

c) Reduce

Example sentence: The medication helped prolong the patient's life.

Rectify:

a) Correct

b) Ruin

c) Mismanage

Example sentence: The company took immediate steps to rectify the error in their billing system.

Respite:

a) Break

b) Continuation

c) Perseverance

Example sentence: After weeks of hard work, she took a well-deserved respite.

Skirmish:

a) Conflict

b) Harmony

c) Peace

Example sentence: The two armies engaged in a skirmish near the border.

Scrutinize:

a) Examine

b) Ignore

c) Neglect

Example sentence: The detective scrutinized the crime scene for any potential evidence.

Group 27:

Amiable:

a) Friendly

b) Hostile

c) Unfriendly

Example sentence: The shopkeeper had an amiable personality, always greeting customers with a smile.

Consensus:

a) Agreement

b) Disagreement

c) Discord

Example sentence: After much discussion, the team reached a consensus on the best approach.

Dormant:

a) Inactive

b) Active

c) Lively

Example sentence: The volcano had been dormant for centuries until it suddenly erupted.

Frivolous:

a) Trivial

b) Serious

c) Important

Example sentence: She spent her time on frivolous activities instead of focusing on her studies.

Innate:

a) Inborn

b) Acquired

c) Learned

Example sentence: Some people have an innate talent for

playing musical instruments.

Prominent:

    a) Eminent

    b) Obscure

    c) Unknown

Example sentence: The professor is a prominent figure in the field of astrophysics.

Rectitude:

    a) Integrity

    b) Dishonesty

    c) Corruption

Example sentence: The politician was known for his rectitude and commitment to ethical practices.

Reticent:

    a) Reserved

    b) Talkative

    c) Outspoken

Example sentence: He was reticent about discussing his personal life with others.

Sluggish:

    a) Lethargic

    b) Energetic

    c) Active

Example sentence: The hot weather made her feel sluggish and unmotivated.

Serene:

    a) Calm

    b) Turbulent

    c) Chaotic

Example sentence: She enjoyed sitting by the lake, enjoying the serene surroundings.

Group 28:

Amicable:

    a) Friendly

    b) Hostile

    c) Unfriendly

Example sentence: They had an amicable discussion and reached a mutually beneficial agreement.

Constraint:

    a) Restriction

    b) Freedom

    c) Liberty

Example sentence: The budget constraints limited the company's ability to expand.

Drastic:

    a) Radical

    b) Mild

    c) Moderate

Example sentence: The company had to take drastic measures to cut costs and avoid bankruptcy.

Frustrate:

    a) Disappoint

    b) Satisfy

    c) Fulfill

Example sentence: The continuous setbacks frustrated their efforts to complete the project on time.

Innovative:

    a) Creative

    b) Traditional

    c) Conventional

Example sentence: The company introduced an innovative

product that revolutionized the market.

Prudent:

    a) Wise

    b) Foolish

    c) Reckless

Example sentence: It's prudent to save money for emergencies.

Revere:

    a) Admire

    b) Disdain

    c) Despise

Example sentence: The community revered the elderly leader for her wisdom and guidance.

Reticent:

    a) Reserved

    b) Talkative

    c) Outspoken

Example sentence: He was reticent about discussing his personal life with others.

Smug:

    a) Self-satisfied

    b) Modest

    c) Humble

Example sentence: His smug attitude annoyed his colleagues.

Serene:

    a) Calm

    b) Turbulent

    c) Chaotic

Example sentence: She enjoyed sitting by the lake, enjoying the serene surroundings.

Group 29:

Amplify:

    a) Increase

    b) Decrease

    c) Diminish

Example sentence: The microphone amplified his voice, making it louder and clearer.

Consummate:

    a) Complete

    b) Incomplete

    c) Partial

Example sentence: The pianist's performance was consummate, displaying exceptional skill and artistry.

Dubious:

    a) Doubtful

    b) Certain

    c) Convinced

Example sentence: The evidence against him was dubious and lacked credibility.

Futile:

    a) Pointless

    b) Effective

    c) Successful

Example sentence: Despite their efforts, their attempts to negotiate a resolution proved futile.

Innovative:

    a) Creative

    b) Traditional

    c) Conventional

Example sentence: The company introduced an innovative

product that revolutionized the market.

Punctual:

a) Prompt

b) Late

c) Delayed

Example sentence: He was known for his punctual arrival at every meeting.

Revoke:

a) Cancel

b) Grant

c) Authorize

Example sentence: The government decided to revoke the driver's license due to multiple violations.

Reverence:

a) Respect

b) Disrespect

c) Contempt

Example sentence: The students showed reverence towards their teacher, treating him with great respect.

Solace:

a) Comfort

b) Distress

c) Grief

Example sentence: She sought solace in her favorite book during difficult times.

Subtle:

a) Delicate

b) Obvious

c) Blatant

Example sentence: The artist used subtle shades of blue to create a calming effect in the painting.

Group 30:

Animosity:

   a) Hostility

   b) Friendliness

   c) Harmony

Example sentence: There was a deep-seated animosity between the rival gangs.

Contemplate:

   a) Ponder

   b) Disregard

   c) Ignore

Example sentence: She sat by the window, contemplating the meaning of life.

Duplicity:

   a) Deception

   b) Honesty

   c) Sincerity

Example sentence: He was known for his duplicity, often saying one thing and doing another.

Gregarious:

   a) Sociable

   b) Introverted

   c) Shy

Example sentence: She was a gregarious person who enjoyed being around others.

Intervene:

   a) Mediate

   b) Ignore

   c) Stay out of

Example sentence: The teacher had to intervene and break

up the fight between the students.

Pungent:

a) Strong-smelling

b) Mild

c) Fragrant

Example sentence: The pungent odor of the onions made her eyes water.

Revitalize:

a) Renew

b) Weaken

c) Exhaust

Example sentence: The new CEO implemented strategies to revitalize the company and increase its profitability.

Rigorous:

a) Thorough

b) Lenient

c) Lax

Example sentence: The training program was rigorous, pushing the participants to their limits.

Soporific:

a) Sleep-inducing

b) Stimulating

c) Energizing

Example sentence: The sound of rain can be quite soporific and help people fall asleep.

Substantiate:

a) Support

b) Refute

c) Disprove

Example sentence: He provided evidence to substantiate his claim.

Group 31:

Anomaly:

   a) Abnormality

   b) Normality

   c) Conformity

Example sentence: The sudden drop in temperature was an anomaly for this time of year.

Contradict:

   a) Disagree

   b) Support

   c) Endorse

Example sentence: His statement seems to contradict the evidence presented.

Eloquent:

   a) Articulate

   b) Inarticulate

   c) Mumbling

Example sentence: The speaker delivered an eloquent speech that captivated the audience.

Hackneyed:

   a) Overused

   b) Fresh

   c) Original

Example sentence: The writer used hackneyed phrases that lacked originality.

Intrinsic:

   a) Inherent

   b) Extrinsic

   c) External

Example sentence: She had an intrinsic talent for playing

the piano.

Pensive:

a) Thoughtful

b) Carefree

c) Unconcerned

Example sentence: He sat in the park, lost in pensive contemplation.

Revive:

a) Renew

b) Terminate

c) End

Example sentence: The paramedics managed to revive the patient after performing CPR.

Rigorous:

a) Thorough

b) Lenient

c) Lax

Example sentence: The training program was rigorous, pushing the participants to their limits.

Soporific:

a) Sleep-inducing

b) Stimulating

c) Energizing

Example sentence: The sound of rain can be quite soporific and help people fall asleep.

Substantiate:

a) Support

b) Refute

c) Disprove

Example sentence: He provided evidence to substantiate his claim.

Group 32:

Antagonize:

    a) Provoke

    b) Pacify

    c) Appease

Example sentence: His aggressive behavior only served to antagonize his opponents.

Contribute:

    a) Contribute

    b) Withhold

    c) Withdraw

Example sentence: Each team member must contribute to the project's success.

Eradicate:

    a) Eliminate

    b) Preserve

    c) Protect

Example sentence: Efforts are being made to eradicate poverty in the region.

Harmony:

    a) Accord

    b) Discord

    c) Conflict

Example sentence: The choir sang in perfect harmony, creating a beautiful musical experience.

Intrepid:

    a) Fearless

    b) Timid

    c) Cowardly

Example sentence: The intrepid explorer ventured into

unknown territory.

Persevere:

    a) Persist

    b) Quit

    c) Abandon

Example sentence: Despite facing numerous challenges, she persevered and achieved her goals.

Revocable:

    a) Reversible

    b) Irreversible

    c) Unchangeable

Example sentence: The contract included a revocable clause that allowed either party to cancel it.

Robust:

    a) Strong

    b) Weak

    c) Fragile

Example sentence: He had a robust immune system that rarely succumbed to illness.

Spontaneous:

    a) Impulsive

    b) Planned

    c) Deliberate

Example sentence: They had a spontaneous gathering to celebrate their achievements.

Subtle:

    a) Delicate

    b) Obvious

    c) Blatant

Example sentence: The artist used subtle shades of blue to create a calming effect in the painting.

Group 33:

Apathy:

    a) Indifference

    b) Interest

    c) Enthusiasm

Example sentence: His apathy towards his studies resulted in poor grades.

Conventional:

    a) Traditional

    b) Unconventional

    c) Radical

Example sentence: They opted for a conventional wedding ceremony with all the traditional customs.

Erratic:

    a) Unpredictable

    b) Consistent

    c) Stable

Example sentence: His erratic behavior made it difficult for others to trust him.

Hasten:

    a) Accelerate

    b) Delay

    c) Procrastinate

Example sentence: They had to hasten their pace to catch the last train.

Intricate:

    a) Complex

    b) Simple

    c) Straightforward

Example sentence: The artist created an intricate design

with fine details.

Pessimistic:

    a) Negative

    b) Optimistic

    c) Hopeful

Example sentence: She had a pessimistic view of the situation, expecting the worst outcome.

Rigidity:

    a) Stiffness

    b) Flexibility

    c) Adaptability

Example sentence: His rigidity prevented him from considering alternative solutions.

Robust:

    a) Strong

    b) Weak

    c) Fragile

Example sentence: He had a robust immune system that rarely succumbed to illness.

Sporadic:

    a) Occasional

    b) Regular

    c) Continuous

Example sentence: The company experienced sporadic sales during the off-season.

Subversive:

    a) Subversive

    b) Loyal

    c) Compliant

Example sentence: The group was involved in subversive activities aimed at overthrowing the government.

Group 34:

Apprehensive:

    a) Anxious

    b) Confident

    c) Assured

Example sentence: She felt apprehensive before taking the exam.

Conviction:

    a) Strong belief

    b) Doubt

    c) Uncertainty

Example sentence: His conviction in his abilities helped him overcome challenges.

Erudite:

    a) Knowledgeable

    b) Ignorant

    c) Uneducated

Example sentence: The professor was highly erudite in the field of literature.

Haughty:

    a) Arrogant

    b) Humble

    c) Modest

Example sentence: She had a haughty demeanor, looking down on others.

Inundate:

    a) Overwhelm

    b) Deplete

    c) Empty

Example sentence: The office was inundated with emails

after the announcement was made.

Petulant:

a) Irritable

b) Patient

c) Tolerant

Example sentence: The child's petulant behavior annoyed his parents.

Rigid:

a) Inflexible

b) Flexible

c) Adaptable

Example sentence: The company's rigid policies stifled innovation and creativity.

Robust:

a) Strong

b) Weak

c) Fragile

Example sentence: He had a robust physique that allowed him to endure physically demanding tasks.

Spurious:

a) False

b) Genuine

c) Authentic

Example sentence: The article contained spurious information and should not be trusted.

Succumb:

a) Yield

b) Resist

c) Overcome

Example sentence: Despite their best efforts, they eventually succumbed to exhaustion.

Group 35:

Arbitrary:

a) Random

b) Intentional

c) Deliberate

Example sentence: The selection process seemed arbitrary, with no clear criteria.

Credible:

a) Reliable

b) Untrustworthy

c) Dubious

Example sentence: The witness provided credible evidence to support her testimony.

Esoteric:

a) Obscure

b) Common

c) Familiar

Example sentence: The book delves into esoteric topics that require specialized knowledge.

Heresy:

a) Dissent

b) Orthodoxy

c) Conformity

Example sentence: His ideas were considered heresy within the established religious doctrines.

Invariably:

a) Always

b) Occasionally

c) Seldom

Example sentence: He was invariably punctual, never

arriving late for appointments.

Philanthropy:

a) Charitable giving

b) Selfishness

c) Greed

Example sentence: The billionaire engaged in philanthropy, donating millions to various causes.

Rigorous:

a) Thorough

b) Lenient

c) Lax

Example sentence: The training program was rigorous, pushing the participants to their limits.

Rudimentary:

a) Basic

b) Advanced

c) Complex

Example sentence: She only had a rudimentary understanding of the subject.

Spurious:

a) False

b) Genuine

c) Authentic

Example sentence: The article contained spurious information and should not be trusted.

Sullen:

a) Gloomy

b) Cheerful

c) Bright

Example sentence: He wore a sullen expression, indicating his unhappiness.

Group 36:

Arcane:

    a) Mysterious

    b) Obvious

    c) Clear

Example sentence: The ancient manuscript contained arcane symbols and texts.

Criterion:

    a) Standard

    b) Exception

    c) Deviation

Example sentence: The main criterion for admission to the program is academic excellence.

Esteem:

    a) Respect

    b) Disdain

    c) Contempt

Example sentence: She held her mentor in high esteem for his guidance and wisdom.

Hierarchy:

    a) Ranking

    b) Equality

    c) Parity

Example sentence: The organization had a clear hierarchy with distinct levels of authority.

Invoke:

    a) Call upon

    b) Ignore

    c) Neglect

Example sentence: The speaker tried to invoke a sense of

patriotism among the audience.

Pivotal:

    a) Crucial

    b) Insignificant

    c) Trivial

Example sentence: The CEO's decision was pivotal in determining the company's future.

Rigid:

    a) Inflexible

    b) Flexible

    c) Adaptable

Example sentence: The company's rigid policies stifled innovation and creativity.

Rudimentary:

    a) Basic

    b) Advanced

    c) Complex

Example sentence: She only had a rudimentary understanding of the subject.

Spurn:

    a) Reject

    b) Accept

    c) Embrace

Example sentence: He spurned the offer, refusing to be a part of their unethical practices.

Supplant:

    a) Replace

    b) Retain

    c) Reinforce

Example sentence: The new technology has the potential to supplant traditional methods.

Group 37:

Archetype:

    a) Prototype

    b) Variation

    c) Modification

Example sentence: The character of the hero is often seen as an archetype in literature.

Cryptic:

    a) Enigmatic

    b) Transparent

    c) Clear

Example sentence: The message was written in cryptic code, difficult to decipher.

Ethereal:

    a) Heavenly

    b) Earthly

    c) Mundane

Example sentence: The ballet dancer moved with an ethereal grace, captivating the audience.

Homogeneous:

    a) Uniform

    b) Diverse

    c) Varied

Example sentence: The group was homogeneous in terms of cultural background.

Irony:

    a) Paradox

    b) Sincerity

    c) Literalness

Example sentence: The irony of the situation was that the

firefighter's house burned down.

Plausible:

    a) Credible

    b) Implausible

    c) Unbelievable

Example sentence: The suspect provided a plausible alibi for the time of the crime.

Riveting:

    a) Captivating

    b) Boring

    c) Tedious

Example sentence: The movie had a riveting plot that kept the audience on the edge of their seats.

Rudimentary:

    a) Basic

    b) Advanced

    c) Complex

Example sentence: She only had a rudimentary understanding of the subject.

Squander:

    a) Waste

    b) Conserve

    c) Preserve

Example sentence: He squandered his inheritance on frivolous purchases.

Surmise:

    a) Guess

    b) Know

    c) Confirm

Example sentence: Based on the evidence, we can only surmise what happened.

Group 38:

Arduous:

    a) Difficult

    b) Easy

    c) Simple

Example sentence: The climbers faced arduous conditions as they reached the summit.

Curtail:

    a) Reduce

    b) Expand

    c) Increase

Example sentence: The government implemented measures to curtail public spending.

Evanescent:

    a) Transient

    b) Permanent

    c) Enduring

Example sentence: The rainbow appeared evanescent, fading away within minutes.

Hypocritical:

    a) Insincere

    b) Genuine

    c) Honest

Example sentence: His actions were hypocritical, contradicting his stated beliefs.

Jeopardize:

    a) Endanger

    b) Protect

    c) Safeguard

Example sentence: His reckless behavior could jeopardize

the success of the project.

Plausible:

    a) Credible

    b) Implausible

    c) Unbelievable

Example sentence: The suspect provided a plausible alibi for the time of the crime.

Robust:

    a) Strong

    b) Weak

    c) Fragile

Example sentence: He had a robust physique that allowed him to endure physically demanding tasks.

Ruse:

    a) Trick

    b) Truth

    c) Honesty

Example sentence: The magician used a clever ruse to deceive the audience.

Squander:

    a) Waste

    b) Conserve

    c) Preserve

Example sentence: He squandered his inheritance on frivolous purchases.

Susceptible:

    a) Vulnerable

    b) Resistant

    c) Immune

Example sentence: Children are more susceptible to catching colds than adults.

Group 39:

Articulate:

    a) Expressive

    b) Inarticulate

    c) Mute

Example sentence: The speaker was able to articulate her thoughts clearly and persuasively.

Deference:

    a) Respect

    b) Disrespect

    c) Contempt

Example sentence: He showed deference to his elders by listening attentively to their advice.

Exacerbate:

    a) Aggravate

    b) Alleviate

    c) Improve

Example sentence: His careless actions only served to exacerbate the situation.

Iconoclast:

    a) Nonconformist

    b) Conformist

    c) Traditionalist

Example sentence: The artist was known as an iconoclast, challenging traditional artistic norms.

Juxtapose:

    a) Compare

    b) Separate

    c) Isolate

Example sentence: The photographer juxtaposed images of

urban life with scenes of nature.

Plausible:

    a) Credible

    b) Implausible

    c) Unbelievable

Example sentence: The suspect provided a plausible alibi for the time of the crime.

Robust:

    a) Strong

    b) Weak

    c) Fragile

Example sentence: He had a robust immune system that rarely succumbed to illness.

Rustic:

    a) Rural

    b) Urban

    c) Metropolitan

Example sentence: They decided to spend their vacation in a rustic cabin in the woods.

Stagnant:

    a) Inactive

    b) Dynamic

    c) Progressive

Example sentence: The company's growth had become stagnant in recent years.

Sycophant:

    a) Flatterer

    b) Critic

    c) Opponent

Example sentence: He surrounded himself with sycophants who would always praise him.

Group 40:

Ascend:

a) Climb

b) Descend

c) Fall

Example sentence: The hiker began to ascend the steep mountain trail.

Defiant:

a) Resistant

b) Compliant

c) Obedient

Example sentence: The student's defiant attitude towards the teacher led to disciplinary action.

Exasperate:

a) Irritate

b) Calm

c) Soothe

Example sentence: The constant noise from the construction site exasperated the residents.

Idealize:

a) Idolize

b) Criticize

c) Disapprove

Example sentence: He tended to idealize his romantic partners, seeing only their positive traits.

Juxtapose:

a) Compare

b) Separate

c) Isolate

Example sentence: The author juxtaposed two contrasting

characters in her novel.

Plausible:

    a) Credible

    b) Implausible

    c) Unbelievable

Example sentence: The suspect provided a plausible alibi for the time of the crime.

Roster:

    a) List

    b) Schedule

    c) Inventory

Example sentence: The coach finalized the roster for the upcoming basketball season.

Ruthless:

    a) Merciless

    b) Compassionate

    c) Kind

Example sentence: The ruthless dictator ruled the country with an iron fist.

Stamina:

    a) Endurance

    b) Weakness

    c) Fatigue

Example sentence: Marathon runners need to have exceptional stamina to complete the race.

Synthesis:

    a) Combination

    b) Separation

    c) Division

Example sentence: The synthesis of art and technology resulted in innovative designs.

Group 41:

Aspire:

 a) Desire

 b) Give up

 c) Abandon

Example sentence: She aspired to become a successful entrepreneur.

Deft:

 a) Skillful

 b) Clumsy

 c) Awkward

Example sentence: The pianist played the intricate piece with deft fingers.

Exemplify:

 a) Illustrate

 b) Contradict

 c) Disprove

Example sentence: The student's project exemplified creativity and innovation.

Illuminate:

 a) Light up

 b) Darken

 c) Dim

Example sentence: The candles illuminated the room with a soft, warm glow.

Malleable:

 a) Flexible

 b) Rigid

 c) Inflexible

Example sentence: The clay was malleable and easy to

shape.

Pragmatic:

    a) Practical

    b) Idealistic

    c) Impractical

Example sentence: The politician took a pragmatic approach to problem-solving.

Rotund:

    a) Round

    b) Thin

    c) Slender

Example sentence: The rotund man struggled to fit into the small chair.

Sagacious:

    a) Wise

    b) Foolish

    c) Ignorant

Example sentence: The sagacious elder provided valuable advice to the young ones.

Tenacious:

    a) Persistent

    b) Inconsistent

    c) Fickle

Example sentence: She displayed tenacious determination in achieving her goals.

Unprecedented:

    a) Unparalleled

    b) Common

    c) Typical

Example sentence: The company achieved unprecedented success in a short period.

Group 42:

Assert:

    a) Declare

    b) Retract

    c) Disavow

Example sentence: The lawyer asserted her client's innocence.

Demeanor:

    a) Behavior

    b) Manner

    c) Attitude

Example sentence: His calm demeanor helped diffuse the tense situation.

Exhaustive:

    a) Thorough

    b) Superficial

    c) Incomplete

Example sentence: The research paper provided an exhaustive analysis of the topic.

Imminent:

    a) Impending

    b) Distant

    c) Remote

Example sentence: The storm clouds indicated that rain was imminent.

Mandate:

    a) Require

    b) Permit

    c) Allow

Example sentence: The government issued a mandate

requiring all citizens to wear masks.

Precarious:

    a) Unstable

    b) Secure

    c) Stable

Example sentence: The hiker carefully balanced on the precarious edge of the cliff.

Sanguine:

    a) Optimistic

    b) Pessimistic

    c) Gloomy

Example sentence: Despite the challenges, she remained sanguine about the future.

Scrutinize:

    a) Examine

    b) Ignore

    c) Neglect

Example sentence: The detective scrutinized the crime scene for any evidence.

Tenuous:

    a) Weak

    b) Strong

    c) Robust

Example sentence: The argument was based on a tenuous connection between the two events.

Unscrupulous:

    a) Unethical

    b) Moral

    c) Honorable

Example sentence: The unscrupulous businessman resorted to illegal tactics for profit.

Group 43:

Assimilate:

a) Absorb

b) Reject

c) Exclude

Example sentence: Immigrants often face challenges as they try to assimilate into a new culture.

Demise:

a) Death

b) Birth

c) Revival

Example sentence: The demise of the company was attributed to poor management decisions.

Exhilarating:

a) Thrilling

b) Boring

c) Dull

Example sentence: The roller coaster ride was exhilarating and filled with adrenaline.

Impartial:

a) Unbiased

b) Biased

c) Prejudiced

Example sentence: The judge made impartial decisions based solely on the evidence.

Mitigate:

a) Alleviate

b) Aggravate

c) Intensify

Example sentence: The organization implemented

measures to mitigate the impact of climate change.

Pristine:

    a) Pure

    b) Contaminated

    c) Polluted

Example sentence: The beach was pristine with clear blue waters and untouched sand.

Scrutiny:

    a) Examination

    b) Neglect

    c) Disregard

Example sentence: The financial statements underwent careful scrutiny by auditors.

Serene:

    a) Calm

    b) Turbulent

    c) Chaotic

Example sentence: The peaceful lake provided a serene atmosphere for relaxation.

Trepidation:

    a) Fear

    b) Confidence

    c) Assurance

Example sentence: She entered the haunted house with trepidation, unsure of what to expect.

Unwarranted:

    a) Unjustified

    b) Justified

    c) Valid

Example sentence: The police conducted an unwarranted search without proper evidence.

Group 44:

Assuage:

    a) Ease

    b) Aggravate

    c) Worsen

Example sentence: He took medication to assuage his severe headache.

Denounce:

    a) Condemn

    b) Approve

    c) Praise

Example sentence: The activist denounced the government's oppressive policies.

Exonerate:

    a) Clear

    b) Blame

    c) Accuse

Example sentence: The DNA evidence helped exonerate the wrongly convicted man.

Incessant:

    a) Unending

    b) Occasional

    c) Intermittent

Example sentence: The incessant noise from the construction site disrupted the neighborhood.

Meticulous:

    a) Diligent

    b) Careless

    c) Negligent

Example sentence: The artist paid meticulous attention to

every detail of her artwork.

Prolific:

a) Productive

b) Unproductive

c) Idle

Example sentence: The writer was known for her prolific output of novels.

Secluded:

a) Isolated

b) Crowded

c) Populated

Example sentence: The cabin was situated in a secluded area, surrounded by nature.

Skepticism:

a) Doubt

b) Belief

c) Conviction

Example sentence: The scientist approached the new theory with skepticism, questioning its validity.

Trivial:

a) Insignificant

b) Important

c) Meaningful

Example sentence: The argument was about a trivial matter and had no real significance.

Utilitarian:

a) Functional

b) Ornamental

c) Decorative

Example sentence: The minimalist furniture had a utilitarian design, focusing on practicality.

Group 45:

Astute:

a) Shrewd

b) Naive

c) Gullible

Example sentence: The astute businessman made profitable investments.

Depict:

a) Portray

b) Conceal

c) Hide

Example sentence: The painting depicted a beautiful sunset over the mountains.

Exorbitant:

a) Excessive

b) Reasonable

c) Moderate

Example sentence: The hotel charged exorbitant prices during peak tourist season.

Indifferent:

a) Apathetic

b) Interested

c) Enthusiastic

Example sentence: She remained indifferent to the outcome of the competition.

Miserly:

a) Stingy

b) Generous

c) Liberal

Example sentence: The miserly old man refused to spend

money on anything unnecessary.

Prominent:

a) Well-known

b) Obscure

c) Unknown

Example sentence: The prominent scientist received a prestigious award for her research.

Severe:

a) Harsh

b) Mild

c) Gentle

Example sentence: The region experienced severe drought, causing widespread crop failures.

Sobriety:

a) Soberness

b) Drunkenness

c) Intoxication

Example sentence: After years of struggle, he finally achieved sobriety and turned his life around.

Truncate:

a) Shorten

b) Extend

c) Lengthen

Example sentence: The editor decided to truncate the article to meet the word count requirement.

Utter:

a) Express

b) Suppress

c) Conceal

Example sentence: She was at a loss for words and could only utter a few syllables.

Group 46:

Asylum:

 a) Refuge

 b) Imprisonment

 c) Captivity

Example sentence: The refugee sought asylum in a neighboring country.

Deride:

 a) Mock

 b) Praise

 c) Applaud

Example sentence: The bullies derided him for his appearance.

Expedite:

 a) Speed up

 b) Delay

 c) Hinder

Example sentence: We need to expedite the process to meet the deadline.

Indulge:

 a) Pamper

 b) Deny

 c) Deprive

Example sentence: After a long day, she liked to indulge in a warm bubble bath.

Mitigate:

 a) Alleviate

 b) Aggravate

 c) Intensify

Example sentence: The company implemented safety

measures to mitigate the risk of accidents.

Prosaic:

    a) Ordinary

    b) Extraordinary

    c) Exceptional

Example sentence: The novel was criticized for its prosaic writing style.

Severe:

    a) Harsh

    b) Mild

    c) Gentle

Example sentence: The doctor advised bed rest due to severe flu symptoms.

Solemn:

    a) Serious

    b) Lighthearted

    c) Playful

Example sentence: The atmosphere in the courtroom was solemn as the verdict was read.

Turmoil:

    a) Chaos

    b) Order

    c) Tranquility

Example sentence: The country experienced political turmoil after the controversial election.

Vacillate:

    a) waver

    b) decide

    c) determine

Example sentence: He vacillated between accepting the job offer and staying in his current position.

Group 47:

Authentic:

    a) Genuine

    b) Fake

    c) Counterfeit

Example sentence: The art expert confirmed the painting to be an authentic masterpiece.

Desolate:

    a) Deserted

    b) Populated

    c) Inhabited

Example sentence: The abandoned house stood in a desolate neighborhood.

Explicit:

    a) Clear

    b) Vague

    c) Ambiguous

Example sentence: The teacher provided explicit instructions for the science experiment.

Indulgent:

    a) Lenient

    b) Strict

    c) Disciplined

Example sentence: The indulgent parents allowed their children to have ice cream before dinner.

Morose:

    a) Gloomy

    b) Cheerful

    c) Happy

Example sentence: He was in a morose mood after receiving

disappointing news.

Proximity:

    a) Nearness

    b) Distance

    c) Separation

Example sentence: The convenience store's proximity to their house made it a preferred choice.

Shrewd:

    a) Cunning

    b) Naive

    c) Gullible

Example sentence: The shrewd negotiator secured a favorable deal for her client.

Solitude:

    a) Isolation

    b) Company

    c) Socializing

Example sentence: He enjoyed the peace and solitude of the mountain cabin.

Ubiquitous:

    a) Pervasive

    b) Rare

    c) Scarce

Example sentence: Mobile phones have become ubiquitous in today's society.

Vague:

    a) Unclear

    b) Precise

    c) Distinct

Example sentence: The witness provided vague details about the incident.

Group 48:

Autonomy:

a) Independence

b) Dependence

c) Reliance

Example sentence: The country fought for autonomy from colonial rule.

Despondent:

a) Depressed

b) Happy

c) Content

Example sentence: The loss of her pet left her feeling despondent.

Fabricate:

a) Invent

b) Destroy

c) Dismantle

Example sentence: The journalist was accused of fabricating the facts in the news article.

Indiscriminate:

a) Random

b) Selective

c) Discriminating

Example sentence: The indiscriminate use of pesticides harmed both pests and beneficial insects.

Mundane:

a) Ordinary

b) Extraordinary

c) Exceptional

Example sentence: He found solace in painting as an escape

from mundane everyday life.

Prudent:

    a) Wise

    b) Foolish

    c) Reckless

Example sentence: It's important to make prudent financial decisions to secure your future.

Shun:

    a) Avoid

    b) Embrace

    c) Welcome

Example sentence: After the scandal, the celebrity was shunned by the industry.

Somber:

    a) Gloomy

    b) Bright

    c) Radiant

Example sentence: The funeral had a somber atmosphere as people mourned the loss.

Unanimous:

    a) Consensus

    b) Divided

    c) Disagreement

Example sentence: The board members reached a unanimous decision on the budget allocation.

Validate:

    a) Confirm

    b) Invalidate

    c) Disprove

Example sentence: The laboratory tests were conducted to validate the research findings.

Group 49:

Aversion:

    a) Dislike

    b) Fondness

    c) Attraction

Example sentence: She had an aversion to public speaking.

Deter:

    a) Discourage

    b) Encourage

    c) Motivate

Example sentence: The high cost of living deterred him from moving to the city.

Facilitate:

    a) Assist

    b) Hinder

    c) Obstruct

Example sentence: The new software will facilitate faster data processing.

Indispensable:

    a) Essential

    b) Dispensable

    c) Unimportant

Example sentence: The internet has become an indispensable tool in our daily lives.

Nostalgia:

    a) Sentimentality

    b) Apathy

    c) Indifference

Example sentence: Looking at old photographs filled him with nostalgia for his childhood.

Pungent:

    a) Strong-smelling

    b) Fragrant

    c) Aromatic

Example sentence: The pungent odor of onions made her eyes water.

Sophisticated:

    a) Elegant

    b) Unsophisticated

    c) Simple

Example sentence: The upscale restaurant had a sophisticated atmosphere.

Somber:

    a) Gloomy

    b) Bright

    c) Radiant

Example sentence: The somber music played at the memorial service touched everyone's hearts.

Unprecedented:

    a) Unparalleled

    b) Common

    c) Typical

Example sentence: The team's success was unprecedented in the history of the sport.

Verbose:

    a) Wordy

    b) Concise

    c) Succinct

Example sentence: His writing style was often criticized for being verbose and lacking clarity.

Group 50:

Banal:

    a) Commonplace

    b) Unique

    c) Extraordinary

Example sentence: The movie had a banal plot with predictable twists.

Deviate:

    a) Diverge

    b) Conform

    c) Comply

Example sentence: She chose to deviate from the traditional career path and pursued her passion.

Fanatic:

    a) Enthusiast

    b) Indifferent

    c) Apathetic

Example sentence: The soccer fanatic painted his face in the colors of his favorite team.

Infallible:

    a) Unerring

    b) Fallible

    c) Imperfect

Example sentence: No one is infallible; we all make mistakes.

Notorious:

    a) Infamous

    b) Unknown

    c) Obscure

Example sentence: The town was notorious for its high

crime rate.

Pensive:

    a) Thoughtful

    b) Carefree

    c) Unconcerned

Example sentence: She sat on the park bench, deep in pensive reflection.

Soporific:

    a) Sleep-inducing

    b) Stimulating

    c) Energizing

Example sentence: The soporific effect of the medication helped him fall asleep quickly.

Sordid:

    a) Disgraceful

    b) Virtuous

    c) Honorable

Example sentence: The scandal revealed the sordid details of the politician's private life.

Unscrupulous:

    a) Unethical

    b) Moral

    c) Conscientious

Example sentence: The unscrupulous businessman cheated his clients for personal gain.

Vibrant:

    a) Lively

    b) Dull

    c) Lifeless

Example sentence: The city's vibrant nightlife attracted tourists from around the world.

REVISION TESTS

U sing revision tests is an effective way to consolidate your understanding of the vocabulary needed for the TOEFL exam. These tests provide you with sentences containing a blank that needs to be filled with the correct word from the provided options. Here's how you can make the most of these revision tests in your TOEFL preparation:

1. Focus on understanding: Read each sentence carefully and try to understand the overall meaning. Pay attention to the context and clues that can help you determine the appropriate word.

2. Identify the blank: Identify the blank in the sentence that needs to be filled with the correct word. Consider the grammatical structure and the intended meaning of the sentence to guide your choice.

3. Analyze the options: Examine the three word options provided for each blank. Pay close attention to their definitions and possible meanings in the given context. Eliminate any options that do not fit the sentence or the intended meaning.

4. Apply process of elimination: Use the process of elimination to narrow down the options. Cross out the words that are clearly incorrect or do not match the context. This strategy increases your chances of selecting the correct answer.

5. Choose the correct word: Select the word that best fits

the sentence and conveys the intended meaning. Ensure that the chosen word aligns with the context and maintains grammatical coherence.

6. Review and analyze explanations: Once you have made your choice, compare it with the correct answer provided. Review the explanations for why the correct answer is the most suitable choice. This step helps reinforce your understanding and provides insights into the usage and nuances of the words.

7. Learn from mistakes: If you make any incorrect selections, don't get discouraged. Use them as learning opportunities. Understand why the chosen word was incorrect and how it differs from the correct answer. This process helps you strengthen your vocabulary knowledge and reduces the chances of repeating similar mistakes.

8. Expand your study: While revision tests are valuable, remember to complement them with other study materials. Incorporate reading practice, listening exercises, and writing tasks that expose you to a variety of vocabulary in different contexts.

Regularly practicing these revision tests will enhance your vocabulary retention, improve your ability to recognize word meanings in context, and boost your confidence when encountering similar questions on the TOEFL exam. Remember to dedicate sufficient time for focused vocabulary study and apply your newly acquired words in real-life scenarios to reinforce your learning. Best of luck with your TOEFL preparation!

Test 1:

The hiker sought _____ in the shade to escape the scorching heat.

    a) solitude

    b) aversion

    c) expedite

The detective's _____ skills helped him unravel the complex mystery.

    a) shrewd

    b) deride

    c) notorious

The student's _____ approach to studying led to excellent academic performance.

    a) prudent

    b) autocracy

    c) turmoil

The chef added a _____ amount of salt to enhance the flavor of the dish.

    a) discerning

    b) mitigate

    c) pungent

The team's _____ victory in the championship was celebrated by their fans.

    a) unprecedented

    b) banal

    c) sporadic

Answers:

    a) solitude

a) shrewd

a) prudent

c) pungent

a) unprecedented

Test 2:

The artist's paintings were characterized by their _____ colors and bold brushstrokes.

    a) vibrant

    b) infallible

    c) autocracy

The team's _____ victory in the tournament secured their spot in the finals.

    a) unanimous

    b) expedite

    c) despondent

The professor delivered a _____ lecture on quantum physics, captivating the students.

    a) verbose

    b) validate

    c) shun

The company implemented strict security measures to _____ any potential data breaches.

    a) mitigate

    b) facilitate

    c) scrutinize

The young boy had an _____ love for animals and dreamed of becoming a veterinarian.

    a) indulgent

    b) notorious

    c) avid

Answers:

    a) vibrant

a) unanimous

a) verbose

a) mitigate

c) avid

Test 3:

The investigative journalist was determined to _____ the truth behind the political scandal.

    a) discern

    b) mundane

    c) expedite

The storm caused _____ damage to the coastal town, leaving many homes destroyed.

    a) indiscriminate

    b) infallible

    c) indifference

The CEO's _____ decision to expand the business led to significant growth and success.

    a) autonomous

    b) soporific

    c) deride

The chef's _____ creation delighted the guests with its exquisite flavors and presentation.

    a) sophisticated

    b) somber

    c) prowess

The athlete's _____ dedication to training paid off when he won the gold medal.

    a) unscrupulous

    b) unprecedented

    c) despise

Answers:

    a) discern

    a) indiscriminate

a) autonomous

a) sophisticated

b) unprecedented

Test 4:

The detective relied on _____ evidence to solve the complex murder case.

    a) validated

    b) verbose

    c) forensic

The team's _____ performance in the championship game secured their victory.

    a) banal

    b) expedite

    c) stellar

The professor encouraged students to _____ different perspectives when analyzing literature.

    a) validate

    b) discern

    c) embrace

The politician's _____ behavior during the debate alienated many potential supporters.

    a) pristine

    b) deride

    c) unscrupulous

The astronaut's _____ experience in space left a lasting impression on his life.

    a) mundane

    b) unprecedented

    c) aversion

Answers:

    c) forensic

    c) stellar

b) discern

c) unscrupulous

b) unprecedented

PARAGRAPH EXERCISES

The exercise involves short paragraphs with blanks that need to be filled with words from the provided lists. Each paragraph presents a context where the appropriate word needs to be selected to complete the sentence. By engaging in this exercise, you can enhance your understanding and usage of vocabulary in meaningful contexts. Here's how you can approach this exercise:

1. Read the paragraph: Begin by reading the paragraph carefully to grasp the overall meaning and context. Pay attention to the tone and subject matter.

2. Identify the blanks: Identify the blanks in the paragraph that need to be filled. Understand the grammatical structure and context to determine the type of word required.

3. Consider the options: Look at the list of words provided after each paragraph. Analyze the options and their meanings. Consider the context and intended message to choose the most suitable word for each blank.

4. Apply process of elimination: Use the process of elimination to eliminate incorrect options. Cross out words that do not align with the context or do not fit grammatically.

5. Choose the correct words: Select the word that best fits the blank, considering both meaning and context. Ensure that the chosen words maintain coherence and convey the intended message of the paragraph.

6. Review the answers: Once you have filled in the blanks, review the provided words and compare them with your selections. Pay attention to the correct answers and understand the explanations for why those words are the most appropriate choices.

This exercise allows you to practice applying vocabulary in context, improving your ability to understand and use words effectively. It also reinforces your understanding of the nuances and meanings of words from the provided lists. By engaging in regular exercises like this, you can enhance your vocabulary skills and boost your confidence in using varied and appropriate language in the TOEFL exam.

Paragraph 1:

The student's _____ dedication to his studies paid off when he received an _____ score on the TOEFL exam. His _____ approach to learning and consistent practice helped him _____ his vocabulary and language skills. He had a _____ desire to improve, and he _____ every opportunity to expand his knowledge. The student's _____ mindset allowed him to overcome challenges and achieve success on the exam.

Words: unprecedented, discerning, aversion, mitigate, vibrant, embraced, autonomous, infallible

Paragraph 2:

The _____ chef prepared a _____ dish using _____ ingredients. The dish was a _____ combination of flavors, and the presentation was _____. The chef's _____ skills and attention to detail were evident in every aspect of the meal. The guests were _____ by the culinary experience and praised the chef's _____ expertise.

Words: sophisticated, discerning, pristine, stellar, avid, captivated, prowess, sophisticated

Paragraph 3:

The community _____ came together to _____ the impact of the natural disaster. Through _____ efforts, they _____ immediate aid to those affected. The _____ support from volunteers and organizations played a crucial role in _____ the suffering of the victims. It was a _____ display of unity and compassion during a challenging time.

Words: disparate, expedite, mitigate, indiscriminate, unprecedented, alleviating, collective, stellar

Paragraph 4:

The young _____ had an _____ passion for music. With his _____ talent, he _____ his own compositions that were both _____ and _____. The audience was _____ by his performance, and he received _____ applause. The musician's _____ dedication and creativity shone through in every note he played.

Words: prodigy, avid, intricate, unprecedented, sophisticated, captivated, resounding, discerning

Paragraph 5: The _____ explorer embarked on an _____ journey to a remote, _____ island. His _____ determination and _____ spirit drove him to overcome numerous challenges along the way. He _____ every obstacle with _____ and found himself rewarded with _____ landscapes and fascinating encounters with wildlife.

Words: intrepid, extraordinary, banal, unwavering, indomitable, conquered, gusto, breathtaking

Paragraph 5:

The _____ scientist conducted _____ experiments to _____ the mysteries of the universe. His _____ research and _____ discoveries revolutionized the field of astrophysics. He _____ every challenge with _____ and had an _____ desire to uncover the secrets of the cosmos. The scientific community _____ his groundbreaking contributions.

Words: intrepid, pioneering, unravel, profound, unprecedented, embraced, tenacity, insatiable, applauded

Paragraph 6:

The _____ activist was determined to _____ change in society. Through _____ efforts and _____ campaigns, she _____ awareness about environmental issues. Her _____ speeches and _____ commitment inspired others to take action. The activist's _____ work made a significant impact on the preservation of the planet.

Words: passionate, incite, relentless, fervent, captivating, unwavering, championed, impassioned

Paragraph 7:

The _____ author crafted a _____ novel that explored the depths of human emotions. Her _____ storytelling and _____ characters captivated readers worldwide. The book received _____ acclaim and was hailed as a _____ piece of literature. The author's _____ talent and _____ imagination were evident in every page.

Words: acclaimed, profound, compelling, vivid, unprecedented, masterpiece, innate, prodigious

Paragraph 8:

The _____ entrepreneur founded a _____ startup that quickly

gained _____ recognition. With her _____ vision and _____ strategies, she _____ barriers and achieved _____ growth in a competitive market. The entrepreneur's _____ leadership and _____ dedication were instrumental in the company's success.

Words: visionary, burgeoning, unparalleled, innovative, pioneering, transcended, exponential, astute, unwavering

Paragraph 9:

The _____ athlete displayed _____ skills in the sporting arena. With his _____ agility and _____ strength, he _____ his opponents and achieved _____ victories. His _____ determination and _____ work ethic earned him _____ respect from his peers.

Words: formidable, unmatched, tenacious, formidable, overwhelmed, unprecedented, unwavering, resounding, adulation

Paragraph 10:

The _____ artist created _____ artwork that evoked deep emotions. Through his _____ strokes and _____ use of color, he _____ a visual language that resonated with viewers. His _____ talent and _____ creativity made him a _____ figure in the art world.

Words: prolific, expressive, bold, mesmerizing, forged, innate, revered, visionary

Paragraph 11:

The _____ architect designed a _____ structure that defied conventions. With his _____ vision and _____ concepts, he _____ boundaries and created a _____ masterpiece. The building's _____ design and _____ integration with the surroundings earned it _____ recognition.

Words: visionary, innovative, groundbreaking, transcended, unprecedented, seamless, awe-inspiring, accolades

Paragraph 12:

The _____ musician composed _____ melodies that stirred the soul. With his _____ talent and _____ compositions, he _____ emotions and created a _____ musical experience. The audience was _____ by his performance, and he received _____ applause.

Words: gifted, haunting, extraordinary, evocative, elicited, transcendent, captivated, resounding

Paragraph 13:

The _____ leader guided his team with _____ and _____. His _____ decisions and _____ strategies propelled the organization to _____ success. The leader's _____ charisma and _____ dedication inspired trust and loyalty among his followers.

Words: charismatic, precision, foresight, astute, innovative, unprecedented, unwavering, unparalleled

Paragraph 14:

The _____ educator had an _____ passion for teaching. With her _____ knowledge and _____ approach, she _____ the minds of her students. Her _____ lessons and _____ enthusiasm created a _____ learning environment.

Words: passionate, ignited, profound, innovative, engaged, infectious, stimulating, nurturing

TSK'S TOEFL VOCABULARY BUILDER

Manufactured by Amazon.ca
Acheson, AB